CO

There can be few better places to walk in lowland England than in the Marches, the borderland country of England and Wales. This is where gentle pastures give way to steeply wooded slopes and open hill tops. Here you will find The Mortimer Trail, a 30 mile walking route from Ludlow to Kington which follows a succession of hills and ridges in a north-east to south-westerly direction. It is so called because this was the very heartland of the Mortimer family, holders of the most powerful of the Norman Earldoms.

Each mile of this Trail holds promise. It passes through forests where tracts of broadleaved woodland give way to coniferous stands. Here you will find deer grazing in the cover of Mortimer Forest or Shobdon Hill Wood. The route descends from the high ridges to the water's edge of the Teme, Lugg and Arrow rivers where Kingfisher and Heron can be seen. Climbs are constantly rewarded by views of the Forest of Radnor, the Black Mountains, Clee Hills and, of course, the majestic Malvern Hills. Pause awhile to admire the worn lines of ancient hillforts and medieval castles holding fast the secrets of previous ages, now the haunt of Buzzard and Jackdaw.

It is a route to be cherished, for there are few such areas so rich in natural history and human heritage. Pass through quietly and you will see and hear wildlife close at hand and preserve the very appeal which makes the area rather special.

For the most part The Mortimer Trail is a high level route away from settlements which are to be found in the gaps and river valleys below. While the hills are rarely over 1,000 feet, you will find climbs which are strenuous in places such as at High Vinnals, Shobdon Hill Wood and Byton.

There are, however, five Loop Walks - Yarpole, Wigmore, Lingen, Shobdon and Titley - which allow you to descend from the ridges to seek refreshment and accommodation or public transport back to a starting point. For example, it is possible to walk out of Ludlow on the main Trail to Croft Ambrey and then head north on the Loop to Wigmore, eventually returning by bus. The Loops also make for splendid circular half day and day walks.

The north west corner of Herefordshire and south Shropshire are characterised by a series of rock formations which give rise to a number of limestone edges.   These dip to valleys where softer shales have been eroded, most probably during post glacial times.

Silurian Trilobite

These rocks were classified in the last century by the famous geologist, Sir Roderick Murcheson, as part of the Silurian System which were formed some 400 million years ago.   There is a fascinating geological trail at Mortimer Forest, known as the Mortimer Forest Geology Trail, which explores and explains the geology and fossil bearing strata of the area.

Most of the upland areas are covered with woodlands, many of which are managed by Forest Enterprise. On The Mortimer Trail, tree cover along several sections has been thinned to encourage a variety of wildlife and to offer improved views.   Ash, Oak, Beech and Lime are common broadleaves. The coniferous blocks are mainly Larch, Douglas Fir and Norway Spruce although others are grown such as the Scots and Corsican Pine.

The Mortimer Trail crosses three beautiful river valleys – the Teme, Lugg and Arrow and their tributaries. The Arrow, which is approached by the Trail near Kington, flows into the Lugg below Leominster. The Lugg in turn joins the River Wye at Mordiford. The Teme flows through to the River Severn near Worcester.

All three rivers rise in the mountains of Powys, although the Arrow soon reaches Herefordshire. They are known to be virtually free of pollution and a stronghold for wildlife. Accordingly, the River Lugg has been designated as a 'Site of Special Scientific Interest' by English Nature, a designation which affords special conservation status. The rivers support a variety of fish including Brown Trout and Salmon, whilst an Otter population has returned to colonise them once more.

For the most part, the Mortimer Trail passes through farmland which is primarily permanent pasture used to fatten stock or rear sheep for sale at local markets. There is very little arable farming except on the lower slopes towards Shobdon and Titley. There are few cider apple orchards in this part of Herefordshire but you will see by some farms small traditional orchards with standard size trees. These have been planted primarily for domestic use.

One significant feature along the Trail is the number of commons. Some, such as Whitcliffe and Bircher, are managed by commoners or graziers whilst others, Byton and Yatton for example, are privately owned. They are used mainly for grazing sheep but local people also enjoy the amenity of these open spaces near to their homes.

The attractive mix of border countryside combined with the relative quiet of many of the hills and valleys makes this an interesting area for the naturalist.

Large areas of woodland combine with parkland rich in veteran trees to support a variety of bird life. Buzzard, Raven and Woodpeckers are numerous and may be encountered year round, whilst more conspicuous summer visitors include Pied Flycatchers and Redstarts. The observant may also be rewarded with views of Crossbill, Peregrine and other birds of prey. Veteran trees are venerable relics that support important insect communities and sometimes house roosts of bats such as Brown Long Eared and Noctule, our largest species.

Other mammals are more conspicuous. Deer at least are likely to be encountered by those moving quietly through the wooded sections. Fallow, Roe and Muntjac are present. More secretive, or nocturnal are Badger, Fox and Polecat, although chance meetings are always an exciting possibilty. Recent evidence even suggests that Pine Martin may still be present in the area.

Roe Deer

The Rivers Lugg, Teme and Arrow suffer little from pollution and consequently are rich in aquatic life including Crayfish, Salmon and Lamprey, and it is always worth keeping an eye out for the electric blue flash of a Kingfisher, or better camouflaged Dipper and Otter. Elsewhere on Commons and open hillsides scarce butterflies and reptiles find their home, along with summering Wheatears and Skylarks.

At various points along the trail there are springtime displays of Bluebells and Ramsons along with a good assemblage of woodland and hedgerow species, and a few scarcer plants to keep the botanists occupied.

One of the joys of the Trail is the visual evidence of past human activity, from the earliest recorded history of hunter-gatherer tribes who lived almost entirely on the high ground to the landscaped parklands set out by our Georgian and Victorian forefathers.

A similar high level route would have certainly been known to ancient tribal groups. Evidence of early settlements can be seen at Croft Ambrey (390BC) and Wapley where there are Iron Age hillforts. Burial cists and mounds have also been found in the area through which The Mortimer Trail passes, in the Lugg Valley and near Kington, for example.

To the Romans, the Marches could best be described as a frontierland as they sought to gain a powerful grip over warring tribal groups such as the Silures. The Mortimer Trail descends to the Lugg Gap (a gorge eroded in post-glacial times) at Aymestrey to cross a Roman road between the garrison towns of Kenchester (Magnis), near Hereford and Leintwardine (Branogenium).

It appears that there was endless warfare in this border region throughout the Dark Ages. Offa's Dyke is a reminder of these times, built by the bretwalda (overlord) 'King Offa', to retain economic and political stability against the Welsh.

Coin of King Offa

The warfare continued through the medieval period and the entire borderland is dotted with the ruins and earthworks of Norman stronghold. Further strife occurred up to and during the English Civil War of the 1640s, although between uprisings life would have continued at it peaceful pastoral pace.

THE MORTIMERS

For four centuries following the Norman Conquest of 1066, the Mortimer family dominated the affairs of the central Marches (the much disputed border area). With land holdings extending from Normandy across southern England and into central Wales, they were to become one of the most powerful and feared families in the land. Theirs is a bloody history of royal alliance, warfare and intrigue. The family seat of power for much of this period was Wigmore Castle, although this shifted later to Ludlow.

The exact date and circumstances under which the Mortimer family under Ralph, acquired Wigmore, remain uncertain, but it appears to have taken place shortly before the completion of the Domesday Book in 1086. He may have defeated "Edric the Wild," the Saxon Earl of Shrewsbury who resisted Norman occupation at Wigmore in 1074.

Wigmore Castle

Certainly William FitzOsbern had built the castle, but the family had fallen from favour when his son entered into a conspiracy against King William (the Conqueror). Mortimer meanwhile was a trusted Norman Baron.

These were troubled, feudal times however and the loyalties of the Marcher barons were fickle, siding both with and against the English Kings in subsequent years, and regularly in conflict with the Welsh, seizing and relinquishing land in successive battles.

There is some evidence that the Mortimers may in fact have been dispossessed of all of their English land under Henry I after siding against him in Normandy only regaining these holdings on the accession of King Stephen, but the historical records for this period are sketchy. In one of the many border skirmishes that followed, it seems Hugh Mortimer was captured by Jose Dinan, another Marcher lord under siege to Hugh at Ludlow. He is said to have paid a ransom for his release of 3000 marks of silver, as well as all his plate, horses and birds, a hefty price indeed. Despite fluctuating fortunes Hugh founded Wigmore Abbey (no longer standing) shortly before his death.

THE MORTIMERS

Subsequent generations added considerably to the families' holdings and power base. Roger, sixth lord of Wigmore, won royal favour with Henry III by rescuing the heir to the throne (Edward) from captivity in Hereford Castle, and later killing Simon De Montford (father of the English parliament) who had taken up arms against the king, at the battle of Evesham. De Montford's head was reputedly sent home as a trophy for Roger's wife, and Roger rewarded by the King with the Earldom of Oxford and a knighthood. In celebration he caused a tournament to be held, at his own cost, at Kenilworth, where he sumptuously entertained a hundred knights and as many ladies, for three days, "the like whereof was never before known in England". Whilst Roger was victorious on this occasion, the family passion for this spectacle was to result in the death of two male descendents in the half century that followed

Roger was also first cousin to his great rival the Welsh Prince Llewelyn ap Griffith and fought against him alongside Edward I. Nevertheless the two cousins are said to have had a considerable mutual respect for one another, but in the year of Roger's death (1282) his four sons tracked down and killed Llewelyn, the last free Prince of Wales.

Roger's grandson, another Roger (b 1287) was to play a leading role in one of the most colourful chapters in the family's history. He was a successful soldier and married well to Joan de Geneville, acquiring Ludlow Castle and extensive Irish estates in the process.

However, he over reached himself staging a revolt against the King (Edward II) and was sentenced to death. He was reprieved but then sentenced to death again and imprisoned in the Tower. Impressively he escaped and fled to France where he pursued a relationship with Edward II's estranged Queen Isabella. Together they formed a powerful alliance and travelled to Holland to negotiate the hand in marriage of her son, the future Edward III in exchange for a small army. With around 3000 men they returned to England in 1326, there many more flocked to their cause and together defeated the unpopular King, who was imprisoned and eventually murdered under mysterious circumstances at Berkeley Castle.

Roger declared himself Earl of March and with Isabella ruled as virtual monarch for four years until the young Edward was old enough to assume the throne. Roger's scandalous behaviour however had roused the anger of other Barons; even his own son described him as the "king of folly." Furthermore the young King still regarded him, probably wisely, as a threat and had Roger arrested and charged with his father's murder. He was subsequently hanged at Tyburn, from the highest gallows.

Four generations later and the Earldom and all the estates confiscated on Rogers execution had been returned to the family, after subsequent

THE MORTIMERS

Ralph Mortimer,
granted Wigmore by William the Conqueror around 1075

Hugh Mortimer,
founded Wigmore Abbey (c.1179)

Roger,
Simon De Montfords nemesis and cousin to Welsh prince Llewelyn (1232-1282)

Edmund,
with his brothers responsible for Llewelyn death

Roger, first Earl of March,
lover of Queens Isabella, dethroned Edward II (1287-1330)

| Roger, Fourth Earl, *chosen by Richard II as his successor (1381-1398)* | Edmund, *plotted with Glyndwr and Hotspur to put the fifth Earl on the throne* | Elizabeth, *married Henry Percy (Harry Hotspur)* |

| Edmund, Fifth Earl *and heir to the throne, died childless, victim of plague in 1425* | Roger | Ann, *married Richard, Edward III's grandson* |

Richard of York

Edward,
*Seventh Earl of March,
crowned Edward IV
in 1461*

Key members of the Mortimer Family ▄▄▄ *indicates generation(s) omitted*

8

generations had nobly supported the monarchy. And so the 4th Earl, yet another Roger, was set to play a significant role. As Richard II had no son to succeed him, he named Roger as his successor. By all accounts it was a popular choice, but this was a dangerous gift in the fourteenth century and Roger was killed during skirmishes in Ireland while Richard remained on the throne.

This still left three male heirs, a daughter and a sister with a legitimate claim to the throne. Richard II's crown was usurped however by Henry Bolingbroke in1399 (Henry IV) and the young Mortimers placed under the guardianship of those loyal to Henry where they could be watched and kept out of harms way. For a while this worked and Edmund, the eldest, who was fearful of Henry made no claim to the throne. Then his uncle, another Edward, was captured in battle and held to ransom by Owen Glyndwr, self proclaimed prince of Wales. Henry's refusal to pay the ransom, or allow other members of the family to raise it, inflamed the anger of Edmund's powerful brother - in - law Henry Percy (Harry Hotspur). Together with Glyndwr and Mortimer they planned to dethrone Henry, put the young Edmund on the throne and divide the rest of the kingdom between them. Henry, however, got wind of the plot and moved swiftly against Hotspur who was defeated and slain at the Battle of Shrewsbury (1403) before the others could come to his aid. This episode is retold colourfully in Shakespeare's Henry IV.

Edmund survived this intrigue but died childless in 1425, and thus ended a spectacularly long male lineage, unbroken for the previous four hundred years. Edmund's second nephew, the 7th Earl of March did however ascend to the thrown as Edward IV after defeating Lancastrian troops in a bloody battle at Mortimers Cross (1461) during the War of the Roses.

The Mortimers played a fascinating part in medieval history but after this their estates and Baronies became merged with those of the crown and Wigmore castle was left to slowly merge back into the peaceful landscape in which it stands today.

HOW TO USE THIS GUIDE

In this guide the main Mortimer Trail route has been divided into 3 sections of between 8 and 11.5 miles. An additional section contains the loop walks.

Within each section there are walking instructions which are cross-referenced by number to the adjacent maps.

The distance and nature of the Trail is indicated, as are other useful details.

When walking please always remember to...

- Tell someone where you are going.

- Wear appropriate clothing and boots. The paths often get muddy and there are climbs and descents which necessitate sturdy footwear.

- Carry adequate clothing in case the weather turns inclement. A small rucksack for a jumper, waterproofs and a snack is ideal.

- Carry a first aid kit. A compass may also be useful and consider a mobile phone if walking alone.

- Follow the Country Code.

- Keep all dogs on a lead.

- Please retain the peace and quiet of the route and be sensitive to local communities and wildlife.

Distance: 8 miles (13km)

Terrain: There are several climbs up to Mortimer Forest and High Vinnals (over 1200 feet). Walking is mainly on forest tracks through to Hanway Common and then along a bridleway to The Goggin. The last section is road walking but these lanes are quiet. **Total ascent:** 2020 ft

Access: Ludlow is well served by trains from Manchester and the North West, Shrewsbury, Hereford and Cardiff. Buses from Birmingham and Hereford stop in Corve Street. The Mortimer Trail is waymarked from both the station and bus stops to Ludlow Castle.

Cut-Off Points:

Richards Castle - From Hanway Common it is possible to walk down to The Castle Inn from where there is a daily bus to Ludlow. 1.5 miles (2.5km)

Orleton Common - From Orleton Common it is possible to walk down to the Maidenhead pub from where there is a daily bus to Ludlow. 1 mile (16km)

Refreshment: There are a number of options in Ludlow but nothing on this section of the Trail unless you divert to Richard's Castle for the Castle Inn, or Orleton where you will find the Maidenhead Inn, The Boot Inn and a village store.

LUDLOW

Ludlow has been described as one of the finest country towns in England. A fortified town laid out in the 12th century, its compact medieval town layout makes it so walkable, and there are half timbered Tudor buildings and Georgian town houses throughout. It is also refreshing to see many small shops in the high streets, and stalls are set out in Castle Square on market day. The town has also gained a reputation for fine food with a number of excellent restaurants and a sizeable annual food and drink festival.

The Castle stands at the top of the Square, a formidable fortification high above the Rivers Teme and Corve. It was founded by the Norman de Lacy family during the 11th century. Then in the 13th century, it passed to the de Genevilles and through marriage to the Mortimers in the early 14th century. The rest of the town prospered as it became the administrative centre for the crown in the troublesome border region.

During the English Civil War the Castle was held by the Royalists and suffered badly until surrendered to the Parliamentarians. From this time it fell into decline, the town however continued to flourish as a fashionable social centre and resort. The castle is open to the public and home to the celebrated Ludlow Festival every summer.

MORTIMER FOREST

This is the name used by Forest Enterprise to describe the various woodlands it manages throughout the central Marches but is also used to describe the main forest of over 1,000 hectares near to Ludlow. There are several woodland trails and numerous events organised throughout the year reflecting Forest Enterprise's approach to recreational use of their land. See also their waymarked 'Geological Trail'.

RICHARD'S CASTLE

From Hanway it is possible to drop down to the scant ruins of Richard's Castle, one of the earliest Norman castles in Herefordshire built by Richard FitzOsbern, hence the name. Standing near to the earthworks is a beautiful Norman church with a detached tower dating from the 14th century. It is no longer the parish church but is open to the public.

ORLETON AND ORLETON COMMON

Orleton Common is a hamlet on the spring line beneath Woodcroft and Patrick's hills. One mile away lies Orleton , a much larger village, where you will find a number of half-timbered dwellings including Orleton Court. Adam of Orleton was born here and as the then Bishop of Hereford he plotted the death of Edward II with Roger de Mortimer.

THE MORTIMER TRAIL

The Route of the Mortimer Trail is subject to constant upgrading and improvement. At times the route may vary from the published map and text.

Any variations in the route will be shown, at the appropriate point, by map boards and waymark signs advising walkers of the revised route.

Whilst every effort has been made to ensure the accuracy of the details given in this publication, neither the publishers nor their agents can be held responsible for any inconvenience arising from or alleged to be caused by any errors or omissions.

1 **The walk commences outside the front entrance to Ludlow Castle - turn right here and follow the path around the castle wall.**

The castle walls have become something of a natural rock garden with masses of Valerian, Yellow Stone Crop and other wild flowers.

The path joins the road shortly; turn right at the T-Junction and cross the River Teme. On reaching the far side of the bridge turn left and then immediately right up a flight of steps onto Whitcliffe Common.

This popular spot is a remnant of a much larger medieval common. The packhorse track which winds its way up from the river, is so called because, according to folklore, it was used by packhorses carrying ore from Clee hill (on the

eastern horizon) to the iron works at nearby Burrington. During the 18th century it became a fashionable promenade.

Where the path next meets the road, turn right. At the hairpin bend continue straight on up the no-through road. After approximately 50 yards take the path left up into the wood. It is worth noting that the route through Mortimer Forest is not marked correctly on the first edition of the ordnance survey explorer map, so it is best to follow the guidebook or signing on the ground.

You are entering the Mortimer Forest here for the first time. During the spring and summer months the cascading song of wood warbler can often be heard here under the shady canopy of oak, sweet chestnut and beech.

2 **On reaching a T-Junction of paths, turn left up to the road, cross over and walk up the drive past the Forestry Commission Offices, continuing straight on into the wood, following the main track over the hill.**

The woodland composition changes dramatically here, to one of mainly conifers with a deciduous fringe. The wide sunny rides are nevertheless excellent for butterflies and dragonflie during the summer months.

3 **Just before reaching the valley bottom you pass a rock exposure, where the path**

1 km
0.5 mile

A49

Ludlow

B4361

Railway
Station

Ludlow
Castle   360 ℹ
Start
①
Weir   Dinham
           Bridge

Whitcliffe
Common

River Teme

North
Farm

Mortimer
Forest
Centre
②
901

Upper
Evens

Lower
Evens

Mary
Knoll

B4361

Mary Knoll Valley   ③ Cliff   Overton

y Knoll
ouse   477

Overton
Common

Sunny Dingle   Wood

leaves the main track next to a cottage. After crossing the stream, turn left onto the main track and then after a few yards turn right up the hill.

There is a nice area of broad-leaved woodland just before you reach the next clearing. Presumably this is how much of this area would have looked before conifer afforestation.

The forest complex is nevertheless an interesting area for wildlife with its mix of mature conifers, clearings and patches of broad-leaves, alongside streams and ponds. Keep an eye out for the longhaired Fallow Deer, for which the area is noted.

4 On reaching a clearing, the route swings around to the right continuing to climb up hill. Cross over the main track and continue over Climbing Jack Common. The path forks left in the plantation above this, on the final approach to High Vinalls.

There are superb views from here over several counties from what is the highest point on the route at 1,222 feet.

Follow the main track over the hill. On reaching the T-Junction turn left and then almost immediately right. After a few hundred yards the path emerges onto Hanway Common; keep to the top of this with the hedge on your right. One hundred yards or so after crossing the farm

drive the footpath veers away from the hedge line. Follow the waymarks down to the corner of the field.

In the spring and summer months red rumped Redstarts often dart along the hedgerows here.

5 At the bottom of the field the route enters an old lane, which leads down to the road. Turn left here and then right up a further road after a hundred yards or so. Take the next road on the left and follow this for about a mile until you come to a T-Junction. After turning right at the junction, continue down to the next road junction and follow the road around to the left signed to Orleton and Leominster.

6 After 50 yards or so take the lane on the right - marked 'Private Drive', and once past a large house look for a footpath on the right which climbs up to meet another road. Turn right here and then follow the road around to the left.

Mary Knoll

Mary Knoll Valley

Overton

cliff

477

4

Overton Common

P

ny Dingle Wood

Haye Park Wood

Tower 1222

Climbing Jack Common

Haye Park House

Hanway Common

link to Richard's Castle

Brush Wood

Vallets

Richard's Castle (remains of)

B4361

5 The Goggin

674

High Cullis

Brighthall Common

Oldfield Farm

Stockin Farm

Cullis Croft

Waterloo House

Orleton Common

406

Woodcock Hill

6 Spout House

The View

Link to Orleton

mile

Lodge

Distance: 11.5 miles (18.5km)

Terrain: The route rises through farmland up to Bircher Common (918 ft) and then is relatively level through to Croft Wood and Croft Ambrey (984 ft). After a gradual descent the route then follows the river valley through Aymestrey to Shobdon Hill, where it climbs steadily to 1070 ft and then descends with spectacular views to Byton village. **Total ascent:** 1887ft

Access: There is a daily bus service 292 to/from Ludlow to the Maidenhead pub in Orleton, which is 1 mile from the route. There is no suitable parking in this area for cars. There is a bus service, Mondays to Saturdays, from Leominster to the turning for Covenhope where a 1.5 mile walk brings you to the Trail at Lyepole Bridge, or to Shobdon where you can join a Loop Walk which brings you to the trail at Shobdon Hill Wood.

Cut-Off Points:
Croft Castle, Aymestrey and Lyepole Bridge

Refreshment:
Riverside Inn and shop in Aymestrey.

CROFT CASTLE

The stone castle at Croft dates originally from the 14th and 15th centuries. It was built on the site of previous fortified structures for the Croft Family who have lived here since the time of Edward the Confessor with a break of 170 years from 1750. The house contains many different styles of interior design, mainly from the 18th century. In the parkland nearby stands a serene little church. Inside, you will find the magnificent tombs of Sir Richard Croft and his wife dating from the early 16th century. The entire Estate is managed by the National Trust and is open to the public.

CROFT AMBREY

Croft Ambrey stands at nearly 1,000 feet and is one of the best examples of an Iron Age hillfort. It is a large, multi-enclosure site which dates from about 390 BC.

LUCTON

From Lucton Common it is possible to walk half a mile down to Lucton village and the school founded in 1708 by a London merchant. Near to Lucton Church and New House Farm is a field path to Mortimer's Cross, by far the best route from The Mortimer Trail to the Mortimer's Cross Inn as you avoid the traffic on the B4362.

MORTIMER'S CROSS

The bloody battle of 1461 took place near to the existing crossroads but the only monument to remind us of this turning point in history is outside the Monument Inn at Kingsland. It was a bitterly cold Candlemas Day in February when Edward (of Mortimer descent) led Yorkist troops to defeat the Lancastrians and hence secured the throne for himself as Edward IV. The Mortimer's Cross Inn and a milestone reflect coaching days of a later era. There is also a water mill by the Lugg which is open to the public, although opening times are limited. The mill also houses a battlefield museum.

AYMESTREY

At a bridging point of the River Lugg on what was a Roman road (now the A4110 here) lies the village of Aymestrey. The Riverside Inn and parish church with surrounding orchards make a very pleasant setting. One of the bells in the church used to be rung each evening to guide bewitched travellers making their way through Pokeshouse (derivation Puck) Wood. A sum of money was set aside by a poor unfortunate soul who had spend a night lost and tormented in these woods but that has long since been exhausted! On the way into Aymestrey you pass by the handsome Georgian building Yatton Court.

SHOBDON HILL AND BYTON COMMON

Wooded Shobdon is nearly two miles long, fringed with Bluebells in the spring the rides are also a good location for deer. Byton is very steep sided and affords wonderful views. Ponies are kept in the upper enclosures. You will see Combe and Byton Moor behind the village, a rare survivor of marshy wetland in the County. The Rivers Lugg and Hindwell can also be seen from here winding their way down the valley from the Radnorshire hills

7 After another 100 yards a path leaves the road on the right and follows the edge of the field.

There are good views behind you here over the fields to the Village of Oreleton.

Continue across several fields keeping the hedgerow on your right and then past some farm buildings keeping to the track ahead. Again keep the field boundary to your right and on reaching the top of the field turn left up to a gate. Once through the gate you are on Bircher Common. Continue straight on for about 30 yards and then turn right. On reaching the open grassland continue straight on towards the conifer wood on the horizon.

Bircher Common is managed by the National Trust. The site is particularly good for a number of species of butterfly. The mass of thistles that decorate the top of the hill during the summer months may be regarded as something of a scourge by graziers but are in fact a superb source of nectar for butterflies and other insects.

8 Enter the wood, then after a quarter of a mile or so take the ride on the right. This is where the one of the loop walks joins. At the top of the bank, go through the gate and turn left.

There is a lovely old Hornbeam just through the gate - in fact there is a row of them along the top of the hill here, this is quite a scarce tree in Herefordshire. The path

follows the outside ramparts of another hill fort here, believed to date from the fourth century BC.

Shortly, you reach a group of pines at the top of the hill where there are fine views to the west. The path follows the slope around to the left, and passes a gate, which offers access to Croft Castle.

Croft Castle and estate are managed by the National Trust. The castle dates from the 14th century and the estate has some wonderful old trees. Both are open to the public and well worth exploring if you have the time.

9 At the end of a row of beeches the route bears left, then turn right on meeting the track.

The barn at the bottom of the track contains an information panel on the Croft estate

Continue through the gate at the bottom of the track and on down the road. Just past the second cottage take a turning on the right which leads up to some fields. Turn right and, once through this field, head across the next field at approximately 10 o'clock and then more or less straight across the next field to the wood. The path continues diagonally right down through Pokehouse Wood, crossing another track before reaching a field at the bottom of the slope. On entering the field turn right at approximately 2 o'clock and continue at a similar angle across the next field.

Woodcock
Hill

The
View

Spout
House

Link to Orleton

406

7

Lodge
Farm

Bircher
Coppice

Yarpole Loop

Whiteway
Head

8

870

Oaker
Coppice

Bircher
Common

Croft
Wood

Stone
Quarry

Leinthall
Common

Lyngham
Vallet

inthall
Earls

Yarpole Loop

Croft
Ambrey
Fort

921

Fishpool Valley

Wigmore Loop

Yatton
Hill

Ladyacre
Plantation

9

1 km

0.5 mile

Croft
Wood

N

A4110

Lucton
Common

B4362

den
use

Yatton
Court

324

10

Pokehouse
Wood

Hill
Farm

PH

Aymestrey
Bridge

558

Ashcroft

PO
Shop

Aymestrey

THE MORTIMER TRAIL

The River Lugg can be heard off to your left - this is the first time we meet this river, which flows from the Radnorshire hills down to the River Wye just south of Hereford

At the next gate follow the track through to the road.

This is Aymestrey. Whilst the route here bears right along the road, the inn and village shop lie a few hundred yards along the road to the left.

10 **Turn right along the road and then almost immediately left. The route now follows this road along the valley bottom for the next mile. Turn left opposite a red brick house and follow the track around to the stile opposite. The route now follows a path along the bottom of Sned Wood through to Lyepole Bridge.**

The secluded reaches of the Lugg support some interesting wildlife. Keep an eye out for Kingfishers, Dippers and Common Sandpipers and if you are really lucky maybe an elusive Otter.

11 **Turn left over the bridge and continue along to the next left-hand bend where the footpath goes straight on up the field. At the top turn left along the forestry track (this is the bottom of Shobdon Hill) from here continue along this track for a quarter of a mile until you reach a gate. Follow the forestry track round to the right and start the ascent of Shobdon Hill. Where the track forks, continue straight on up the slope.**

The woodland on the hill is mostly coniferous and supports a good population of deer, both Fallow and Roe.

At the next fork in the track take the left option.

Until the trees grow back, the clearing at the top of the hill provides some fine views. On the southeast horizon you can pick out the Malvern Hills and to the northeast the profile of the Shropshire Hills.

12 **The next major junction on the left is where the loop walk down to Shobdon village leaves the trail. The trail itself continues straight on. Where the track swings sharp left, take the path off to the right. After another couple of hundred of yards the path branches off left onto Byton Common and follows the top of the slope.**

After a short distance the view opens out over the Lugg Valley with the town of Presteigne at the far end and the distinctive profile of the Whimble poking its head above the surrounding Radnorshire Hills.

13 **At the next T-Junction of paths turn right along the edge of the wood, go through the gate at the bottom and shortly past the first house some steps on the right climb up into a field, continue to the gate opposite. Turn right at the road and continue down past St. Mary's Church to the T-Junction where you turn left**

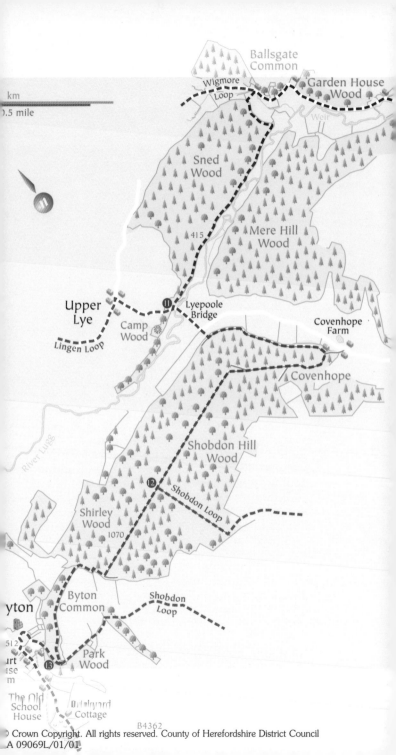

Ballsgate
Common

Garden House
Wood

Wigmore
Loop

Weir

Sned
Wood

Mere Hill
Wood

415

Upper
Lye

⑪ Lyepoole
Bridge

Covenhope
Farm

Camp
Wood

Covenhope

Lingen Loop

Shobdon Hill
Wood

River Lugg

⑫

Shobdon Loop

Shirley
Wood

1070

Byton
Common

Shobdon
Loop

yton

512

Park
Wood

⑬

rt
se
m

The Old
School
House

Oatelyard
Cottage

B4362

km

0.5 mile

Section 3

BYTON TO KINGTON

Distance: 10.5 miles (17 km)

Terrain: After a short road section, there is a hard climb up to Wapley Hillfort, (1059 ft) and then gentle walking through farmland to Titley. Climb out of Titley to Green Lane Farm then fairly level walking along a green lane and the wooded Little Brampton Scar, (1,074 ft) to Knill Garraway Wood. There is another short ascent to Rushock Hill Common, (1,160 ft) before descending through farmland to Kington. **Total ascent:** 2065 ft

Access: There is a bus service, Mondays to Saturdays, from Leominster to Shobdon where you can join a Loop Walk which brings you to the trail at either Shobdon Hill or Byton. There is a limited bus service between Titley and Kington. There are six buses daily (except Sundays) between Kington and Hereford where a train can be caught back to Ludlow.

You will find a small amount of car parking in Titley and there is also a car park at Wapley. There are several car parks in Kington.

Cut-Off Points: Byton (for Loop Walk to Shobdon) and Titley.

Refreshment: Horseway Herbs tea room (half mile detour to Horseway Head) Stagg Inn, Titley and several options in Kington.

BYTON

This small hamlet, mainly comprising of farms, is typical of deep rural Herefordshire. The trail passes near Byton's small church, which is situated above an orchard and offers good views. The church has a tympanum with an early Agnus Dei (Lamb and Flag) above the door.

WAPLEY HILL

Like Croft Ambrey, Wapley was a reasonably large hillfort (pictured) with several enclosures. It covers 25 acres on this high ground. Part of the site has been cleared of trees to conserve the earthworks and this has exposed splendid views across the County. There are waymarked routes through the forest managed by Forest Enterprise.

STANSBATCH

The hamlet of Stansbatch is home to a small nursery. Those wishing to divert by way of Horseway Herbs (and tea room) can do so here or at Lower Mowley. On leaving the hamlet you pass the abutments of the one time Titley Junction to Prestieigne railway, a very late railway which opened in 1875 but closed to passengers in 1951 and to freight in 1964.

TITLEY

In Norman times there was a priory in the environs of the village, an outpost of a Benedictine order from Tiron Abbey in France. It is chronicled that the roadside well by the present church was channelled from water which served the priory and some say that the waters have medicinal properties, although the warning notice on the well is sufficient to ward off would be imbibers. Titley Church is mainly a Victorian restoration. Here you will find the grave of a Hungarian general, Lazar Meszarios. Having been exiled from his own country he called to visit a good friend at Eywood, a stately home near to the village. Unfortunately, he succumbed to a fatal illness and was buried here. Titley Court, at the south end of the village, is an impressive building dating from the mid 19th century.

KINGTON

A traditional gap town on the banks of the infant Arrow, Kington is still very much a market and meeting place for the local farming community. The church stands at the top of the town by the earthworks of Kington Castle. In it lies the tomb of Thomas and Ellen Vaughan, who resided at Hermits Court, much associated with The Red Book of Hergest and local folklore including inspiration for Conan Doyle's "Hound of the Baskervilles". Hergest Croft, with exceptional gardens, parkland and a conservatory, is a ten minute walk out of town on Offa's Dyke Path.

Kington retains a traditional High Street, and next to the Market Hall is the old market place where stalls are set out. Adjacent is the town museum. Kington has justifiably gained a reputation as a walkers' centre - the Offa's Dyke Path meets the Mortimer Trail here and there is a fine network of paths around the town for those seeking shorter walks.

14 Follow the road for a quarter of a mile or so to the crossroads, turn right then first left signed to Wapley Hill Fort. After a further hundred yards the route leaves the road on the right up a flight of steps onto Wapley Hill. The route crosses the corner of a field towards the top of the hill and then continues along the woodland edge. At the next T-Junction of paths turn left and then right after 50 yards. At the end of an avenue of Western Red Cedar take a narrow path off to the right. This emerges at the edge of the hill fort; turn left here.

Four sets of ramparts protect this eastern flank of one of the most substantial hill forts in the county. No excavation has taken place but the design suggests that it may date from the middle Iron Age (c 400 - 100 BC)

15 The route now crosses several tracks as it descends the hill, passing through an area of Beech before reaching a field edge. Descend the field at approximately 7 o'clock to the gate.

The route then crosses a narrow meadow next to a house before reaching the road. Continue on down the road to a T-Junction and turn right, then left after 75 yards. Follow this lane which turns into a path. On reaching the first field bear right cutting across the corner. Head across the next field at approximately 10 o'clock to the stile and turn right at the road.

16 Just past some farm buildings - turn left off the road, then walk right through a field gate and cross the field to a stile in the opposite hedgerow. After crossing the stile bear left around the edge of the field and follow this around until it eventually meets the road. Turn right along the road. After 100 yards or so the route leaves the road on the left, next to a large Oak tree, and heads diagonally across the field to the road. Here we arrive at the village of Titley. Turn left along the road for 50 yards, the main route then leaves the road on the right. (However for the loop walk or the village pub continue along the road.)

Continue along the headland of the next two fields. At the top of the second field the hedgerow swings around to the left. Follow this around and shortly there is a gap in the hedge on your right. Pass through this and cross another two fields heading towards the left hand corner of the second field. Turn left into the lane and then immediately right past some farm buildings.

17 Continue on this track along the ridge, passing through two field gates and then just past an old stone barn turn left through another field gate and walk along the top hedge line. At the far corner of the field the path continues straight along the edge of a wood. Just before a further field gate the path

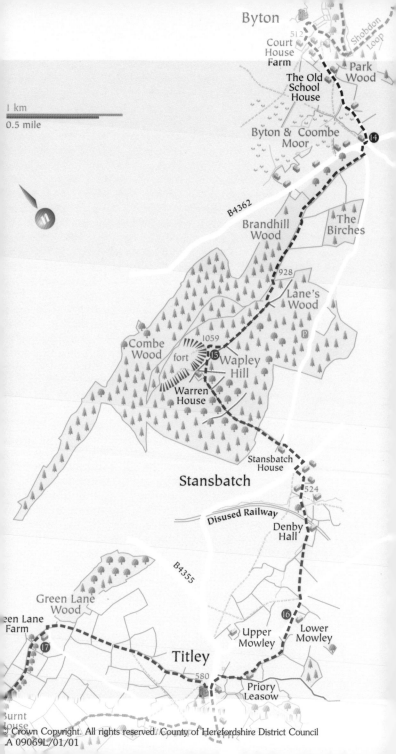

Byton

Court House Farm

512

Park Wood

The Old School House

Byton & Coombe Moor

14

B4362

Brandhill Wood

The Birches

928

Lane's Wood

P

Combe Wood

1059

fort

15

Wapley Hill

Warren House

Stansbatch House

Stansbatch

524

Disused Railway

Denby Hall

B4355

Green Lane Wood

Green Lane Farm

17

16

Upper Mowley

Lower Mowley

Titley

580

Priory Leasow

Burnt House

1 km

0.5 mile

N

Shobdon Loop

heads off right into a field, again continue along the top fence line. At the far side re-enter the wood.

Where the path passes through conifers there is an abundance of Stinkhorn fungi during the summer months. The unpleasant odour is produced by the fungi to simulate the smell of rotting flesh! to attract flies which in turn spread the fungi's spores.

18 Eventually the path descends some steps to join another forestry track, turn left here. After 75 yards turn left, then shortly you enter a field where you follow the left-hand fence line. Crossing a stile at the top of the field follow the track up onto Rushock Hill and aim for a gap in the bank head.

This bank is actually a section of Offas Dyke - of which there is more information in the introduction to this guide.

Continue walking at an angle of 11 o'clock to the Dyke. On reaching a series of undulations, which are actually old quarry workings, turn right towards a gate and stile.

On a clear day there is a good view of the full length of the Black Mountains from here, as well as much of Herefordshire and beyond.

From here the route continues along much the same line, towards the far corner of the field. Follow the road down to a T-Junction and turn right and then almost immediately left up into the field. Follow the left-hand edge of the field until a gate appears on your left and then descend the track. Just before reaching some farm buildings a path climbs the bank on the left towards a stile. Negotiate this and turn right down the field edge. At the end of the hedgerow turn diagonally right and cross the driveway to the opposite hedgerow and descend this to the gate below. The path then crosses the right hand of the two fields, again diagonally to the corner opposite.

19 Cross the road and continue up the track. Shortly after crossing a stream the path leaves the track on the right, crosses a bridge and then heads for the hedgerow opposite. Continue along more or less the same line down the length of the field ahead. After crossing a stile keep the garden hedgerow on your left and shortly enter a driveway, which leads to the road. Turn left at the road, and continue up to the roundabout. Cross the road and follow the signs to Kington town centre.

20 Victoria Road leads into the High Street, where this swings around to the right. Mill Street continues straight on. The trail ends at Mill Street Car Park.

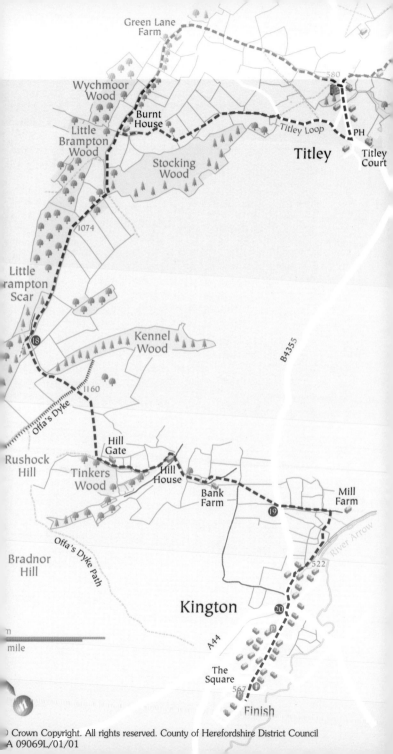

Green Lane Farm

Wychmoor Wood

Burnt House

Little Brampton Wood

Stocking Wood

Titley Loop

PH

Titley

Titley Court

1074

Little Brampton Scar

Kennel Wood

B4355

18

1160

Offa's Dyke

Rushock Hill

Tinkers Wood

Hill Gate

Hill House

Bank Farm

19

Mill Farm

River Arrow

Offa's Dyke Path

Bradnor Hill

Kington

522

20

A44

The Square

567

Finish

Section 4

THE LOOP WALKS

YARPOLE

The parish church, which is surrounded by a group of substantial yew trees, has an unusual detached 13th century bell tower. It stands within a central core of the village, which is a conservation area, with half timbered and other red brick cottage dwellings lining its main street.

Fishpool Valley is designated as a 'Site of Special Scientific Interest' reflecting the rich wildlife which has developed around the decaying fishpools. See the main Trail for details about Croft Castle and Bircher Common.

WIGMORE

Wigmore was in medieval times a significant borough in the Marches and the ruins of its extensive castle and the grand early Norman church standing on high ground evidence this. Both are accessible to the public. Nearby in the Vale of Wigmore stood Wigmore Priory where it is said that many of the Mortimer family are buried. The scant remains are now incorporated into Grange Farm which is private. Wigmore was the home of the Mortimer Family and affairs of state were discussed at Kings Council which were sometimes held here. Pick up the 'Welcome to Wigmore' leaflet which tells you more about the village, its history and the crafts produced hereabouts.

For details about Aymestry and Croft Ambrey see main Trail

LINGEN

This was at one time an influential manor held by the Lingen family and the remaining earthworks of Lingen castle can be seen behind the pretty little parish church. There is an alpine nursery in the village, which is open from February to the end of October. The walk also passes the fine Georgian building of Lingen Hall, which sits above the rippling waters of the Lime Brook.

LIMEBROOK PRIORY

This was a nunnery established by Ralph de Lingen in the latter part of the 12th century. The 16th century cottage nearby is said to have been built with some of the remaining stones from the nunnery. Only one short section of wall remains in a field by the road.

SHOBDON

Shobdon church lies well away from the main village near to Shobdon Court. The existing church was built on the orders of Lord Bateman in the 1750s. He had most of the old church demolished except for the tower and the font, which are still in the present church. The Romanesque style Arches were removed and can now be seen at the head of an avenue of trees. The present church is renowned for having the finest Gothic-style interior in the country. Much of the old Court was demolished in 1933 but you can see the surviving buildings by the church including the impressive stable block.

A guide to walking in the area has been produced by Richard Morley Parish Footpaths Officer) and is available locally.

THE YARPOLE LOOP

Distance: 5 miles (8 km)

Terrain: Easy going with a steady climb up to Croft Wood. Mainly paths and tracks with some road walking between Yarpole and Croft Castle.

Waymarking: Please note that there are no waymark posts on Bircher Common so please follow the map and instructions in the guide.

Access: There is limited on-street parking in Yarpole and at Croft Castle where people are welcome to walk along established paths in the grounds or to visit the Castle when open.

Refreshment: The Bell Inn and village shop at Yarpole offer refreshment.

Commencing at the Bell Inn...

1 From the Bell Inn turn left along the road past the church and at the village shop turn left and continue to the next junction on the left.

Just a few yards after turning left, there is a stile on your right, which enters the field. Follow the hedgerow along; initially on your left then after the next stile with the hedgerow on your right.

Head straight across the next field and then diagonally right across the following field to a stile on the edge of a caravanning field. Cross this to another stile on the edge of the road.

2 Turn left along the road and after a few hundred yards take the no through road sign to Leys Lane on your right.

After three quarters of a mile you cross a cattle grid on the edge of Bircher Common.

There is a nice specimen of a Black Poplar alongside the road just past the cattle grid.

Turn left and follow the track up the slope. Shortly after it swings left take the track off to the right opposite a black and white cottage.

3 On reaching the trees at the edge of the common, turn right and follow the path to the edge of a conifer plantation, where it again swings left. Follow this, crossing another track, then continue onto the open common and follow the line of Gorse straight ahead of you

On a clear day there is a particularly good view of Clee Hill in Shropshire off to the east from here.

Just before reaching the fenceline ahead turn left. The loop walk joins the main spine of Mortimer Trail here. Continue straight on towards the conifer wood on the horizon.

Leinthall
Earls

Leinthall
Common

Whiteway
Head

Croft
Ambrey
Fort

4

Croft
Wood

870

Oaker
Coppice

Bircher
Coppice

Croft
Castle

Fishpool Valley

Croft
Lodge

5

Bircher Common

3

Quarry

497

Woodend
Farm

Clee
View

Old
Rectory

B4362

Cock Gate

Four
Winds

Leys
Farm

Stone
Cottage

Brook
House

Yarpole

1

The Bell Inn

Bircher
Hall

2

Bircher

312

Pound
House

Home
Farm
Campsite

B4362

1 km

0.5 mile

Bircher Common is managed by the National Trust. The site is grazed and managed for nature conservation.

The mass of thistles that decorate the top of the hill during the summer months may be regarded as something of a scourge by graziers but are infact a superb source of nectar for butterflies and other insects.

Enter the wood then after a quarter of a mile or so, where the main spine turns right up to Croft Ambrey, proceed for a few more yards and then turn left off the track.

4 Cross another forestry track continuing down the narrow path through the woods and into the Fishpool valley. At the next fork take the right-hand option, then where the track forks again take the left path.

There are some spectacularly tall trees here notably Douglas Fir, Larch and Ash.

At the next fork, take the left track, just before the path emerges on a tree lined driveway, take another path down to your left.

After crossing a footbridge the path swings right through some woodland to a stile. Negotiate this and walk diagonally left up the slope towards a stile on the edge of the road opposite.

5 Turn right and walk down to the road junction, cross over and continue straight on into the village and back to the Bell Inn.

THE WIGMORE LOOP

Distance: 10 miles (16 km)

Terrain: Steady climbs through the Wigmore Rolls but otherwise easy going with the exception of one major climb through Pokeshouse Wood and an equally steep descent from Croft Ambrey to Yatton. Return 2 mile section is along roads.

Access: There is a daily bus from Ludlow to Wigmore except Sundays. There is limited car parking in Wigmore.

Refreshment:
The Compasses Hotel and Ye Olde Oak Inn in addition to the village store at Wigmore. The Riverside Inn and village store at Aymestrey.

Commencing at the Compasses Hotel...

1 **From the Compasses hotel turn left and follow the road east. Continue along this road for about a mile. When you reach a sign for Leinthall Starkes turn right. After a further mile you reach a T Junction where you turn right again. After a few hundred yards the path leaves the road on the left.**

2 **Follow the edge of the field around to a bridge and continue along the edge of the next field with the hedgerow on your right. At the end of this field turn right along the lane. Turn left when you reach the road and follow for half a mile, then on a sharp left-hand bend turn right up a steep track. At the cottage head through the gate.**

On the right after a few yards is a mature Elm, a very unusual sight in the county, most succumbing to Dutch elm disease before reaching maturity.

Follow the waymarked route towards the right hand group of pines at the top of the hill, where there are fine views to the west. The route goes right here and follows the slope around passing a gate which offers access to Croft Castle.

Croft Castle and estate are managed by the National Trust. The castle dates from the 14th century and the estate has some wonderful old trees. Both are open to the public and well worth exploring if you have the time.

3 **At the end of a row of beeches the route bears left and then turns right on meeting the track.**

There is a National Trust information panel in the barn at the bottom of the track with more information on Croft Ambrey

Continue through the gate at the bottom of the track and on down the road. Just past the second cottage take a turning on the right which leads up to some fields. Turn right and once through this field head across the next field at approximately 10 o'clock and then more a less straight across the next field to the wood. The path continues diagonally right down through Pokehouse Wood, crossing another track before reaching a field at the bottom of the slope,

587

Barnett
Wood

Oakley Hill
Wood

Woodhampton
Wood

5

Lower
Lye

Lye
Court

Sned
Wood

New
Plantation

Loop Walk

River Lugg

367

Ballsgate
Common

Weir

Mere Hill
Wood

Garden
House
Wood

A4110

Garden
House

PH

324

Aymestrey
Bridge

4

PO
Shop

Aymestrey

Pokehouse
Wood

558

Lucton
Common

Hill
Farm

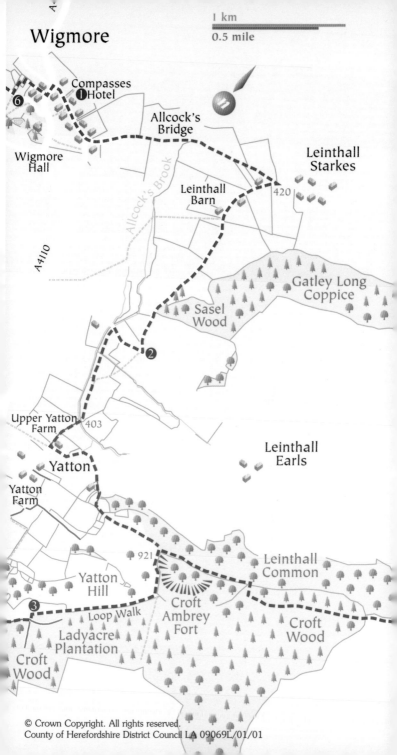

Wigmore

1 km
0.5 mile

6

Compasses
Hotel
1

Allcock's
Bridge

Leinthall
Starkes

Wigmore
Hall

420

Leinthall
Barn

Allcock's Brook

A4110

Gatley Long
Coppice

Sasel
Wood

2

Leinthall
Earls

Upper Yatton
Farm
403

Yatton

Yatton
Farm

921

Yatton
Hill

Leinthall
Common

3

Loop Walk

Croft
Ambrey
Fort

Croft
Wood

Ladyacre
Plantation

Croft
Wood

THE WIGMORE LOOP

On entering the field turn right at approximately 2 o'clock and continue at a similar angle across the next field.

The River Lugg can be heard off to your left, which flows from the Radnorshire hills down to the River Wye just south of Hereford

4 At the next gate follow the track through to the road.

This is Aymestrey. Whilst the route here bears right along the road, the inn and village shop lie a few hundred yards along the road to the left.

Turn right along the road and then almost immediately left. The route now follows this road along the valley bottom for the next mile. Where the spine leaves the road continue along the road for a further half a mile until you reach a farm on a left hand bend, with a trackway going off on the right. The route leads off along this trackway. Where the track forks take the right fork.

5 At the end of the lane enter the field and cross just above the line of Oaks. Follow the slope around to a stile visible at the left hand end of the fence line ahead. Walk the length of this field to a stile in the far right hand corner.

There are a few interesting examples of pollarded oaks in and around this field.

This ancient technique involves felling the trees above head height to protect regrowth from grazing.

Turn right along the road until you reach the end of the wood on your left, where a stile in the hedgerow leads into the field. Head up the slope at 2 o'clock to the stile towards a gate in the top right hand corner of the field.

Enter this next field and turn right towards a stile near the corner. Head across the middle of the next field towards the valley bottom. On reaching the fenceline follow it along to your left until you come to a stile on your right. Negotiate this and turn left, which leads to a footbridge. Once over this head diagonally right up the slope to a stile and gate in the top fence line. Turn right along the road for a hundred yards or so and then left over a stile into a field.

Wigmore Village and its castle come into view here. The romantic ruin and peaceful village below belies its dramatic past as the centre of power in the Marches.

6 Keeping the hedgeline on your right follow this down to a further stile and keep to the hedged in path down to the valley bottom. Turn right here up to the road, turn left for 50 yards or so, and then right down the next road, which leads to the Compasses Hotel.

THE LINGEN LOOP

Distance: 5.5 miles (9 km)

Terrain: The walk is mainly gentle climbs with a steep ascent at Knoll Plantation. There is a mile or more road walking between Lingen and Knoll.

Access: There is a very limited bus service. Car travellers are best to approach from Combe near to Presteigne or from Wigmore. There is limited parking near to the church or the pub.

Refreshment:
The Royal George pub at Lingen.

Tea Rooms at Lingen Nursery and Gardens.

Commencing at Lyepole Bridge...

1 Turn right out of the parking area and follow the road up the hill. At the top follow the road round to the left and after another few hundred yards, turn off the road right, through a gate into a Forestry Commission plot called Knoll. Where the path forks, take the upper path which shortly swings around to the right.

In the summer months this track is alive with butterflies, most notably Meadow Brown and Ringlet.

At the next sharp bend in the track take the narrower path off to the right.

On reaching the gate, turn left up an old sunken lane.

There are some nice examples of coppiced hazel here on both sides of the field, the remnants of an old hedgerow.

2 Turn left when you reach another track, follow this track for half a mile or so until you reach a road. On reaching this, turn left on another gravel track and after 50 yards or so go through the bridle gate and continue down the grassy lane. Turn right down the second track on your right. Shortly the track splits. Take the sunken lane which continues on the right. Continue through another bridle gate and then turn left at a T-Junction.

At the top of a short sharp hill climb take the path off to the left through a field gate. You are aiming for an old fence line opposite here, which leads onto a track which climbs over the brow.

A bit of a curiosity, there are sometimes Rhea, Ostrich like birds from South America, in amongst the sheep here.

3 On entering the field, bear slightly right down into the dip by the fence line, negotiate the stile into the wood and follow the track downhill to the left. At the bottom of the hill turn left.

THE LINGEN LOOP

(The spur off to Lingen Village turns right here - see postscript) At the top of a short incline the path bears right into the grounds of Lingen House. Keep to the tree line on the left. Once past the house you re-enter the wood.

Ramsons line the path here in the spring, and a little further on the lovely blue Nettle Leaved Bell Flower appears during the summer months.

On reaching the bridle gate, turn right down to the farm and right again along the road. Turn left at the next road junction.

4 The remains of Lingen Priory are on the left here.

The route now follows the road back to Knoll plantation. Follow the signs to Upper Lye and Aymestrey. This is where the route originally left the road and from here you can retrace your steps down to Lyepole Bridge.

Spur to Lingen Village...

Follow the grassy track for 100 yards or so and then turn left over the first of several bridges over the Lime Brook and its tributaries.

On reaching a bridle gate turn right over a stile and after crossing a further bridge, turn left along the field edge. This soon passes through a gap in a hedgerow and crosses another small field before reaching the road in the village.

Lingen

The Royal George (PH)

506

Oldcastle Wood

Grove Head

❸ Lingen Hall

Red Wood

Deepmoor Farm

Limebrook Priory (remains) ❹ Old Mill

Limebrook Wood

Lime Brook

Pritchard's Yeld Wood

River Lugg

410

Haven Plantation

862

The Camp ❷

Knoll Plantation

Yeld Wood

533

Bach Brook Farm

Upper Lye

Shirley Wood

Upper Lye Farm

Lye Corner

Camp Wood

Lyepoole Bridge

388 ❶

Shobdon Hill Wood

Mere Hill Wood

Covenhope

1 km

0.5 mile

THE SHOBDON LOOP

Distance: 5.5 miles (9 km)

Terrain: There is a steady ascent to Hill Barn near Byton and a stiff climb up Byton Common to Shobdon Hill Wood. Mainly follows footpaths with some forestry tracks.

Access: Shobdon is served by buses from Leominster on Mondays to Saturdays. There is car parking in the village.

Refreshment: Shobdon has The Bateman Arms, a village store, and a number of other shops and a garage.

Commencing at the Bateman Arms...

1 Turn right out of the pub and after 50 yards turn left through a set of wrought iron gates. This is the approach to Shobdon Church and Court.

Once past the church cross the driveway and continue up the grassy tree-lined avenue.

The avenue is made up of older English Oaks and younger North American Oak. At the top of the avenue are the remains of the Romanesque Arches from the former church. Some interpretation panels describe well the history.

2 Turn left at the arches along the field edge for 40 yards, and then take a track right through the wood for a short distance. When this meets the road turn left.

After a quarter of a mile take the road off to the right, and at the top of the lane continue around to the left through the Forest Research Centre gates. Be sure to close these to prevent deer from entering.

Shortly take the left fork and continue through the gate, then bear right up the surfaced track onto Shobdon Hill. Continue on this track upwards until it eventually meets a T-Junction on top of the hill (this is the main spine route). Turn left here and continue straight on.

3 Where the track turns sharp left, take the path off to the right. After another couple of hundred of yards the path branches off left onto Byton Common. Keep to the fence line along the top of the common here.

After a short distance the view opens out over the Lugg Valley with the town of Presteigne at the far end and the distinctive profile of the Whimble poking its head above the surrounding Radnorshire Hills.

At the foot of Byton the Loop Walk branches off. Turn left, negotiate the stile and continue along the bottom edge of the field. On reaching the far corner, cross the farmyard negotiating a stile on the other side, then walk up to the fenceline and follow this over the brow of the hill down into a wooded valley.

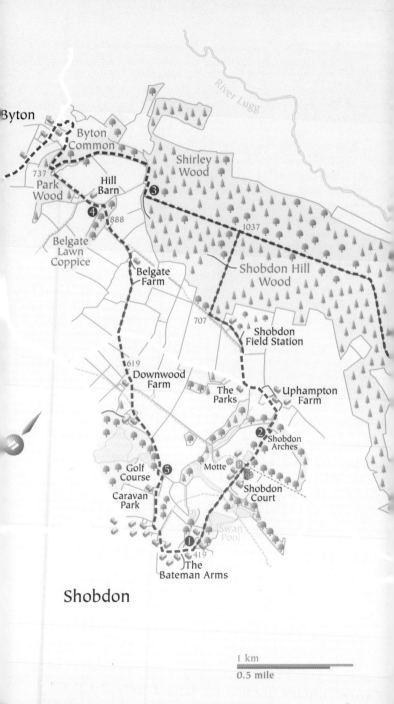

Byton

Byton
Common

Shirley
Wood

737

Park
Wood

Hill
Barn

④

888

③

1037

Belgate
Lawn
Coppice

Belgate
Farm

Shobdon Hill
Wood

707

Shobdon
Field Station

619

Downwood
Farm

The
Parks

Uphampton
Farm

② Shobdon
Arches

Golf
Course

⑤

Motte

Caravan
Park

Shobdon
Court

① Swan
Pool

419

The
Bateman Arms

Shobdon

1 km
0.5 mile

In the spring clumps of Toothwort can sometimes be seen flowering next to the Hazel stumps here. This unusual parasitic plant has no green pigmentation.

4 The path then winds it way right up the wooded bank. On reaching the field the path heads diagonally right and then left through a gate. Continue along the edge of the field keeping the fence on your right. The path continues into a second field and then drops right. Keep the buildings on your left and follow the drive, which after quarter of a mile reaches the road.

Cross over the road and continue to the stile opposite. From here head across the next field at an angle of about eleven o clock to a stile in the hedge. Cross this and walk along the fenceline until you come to a stile on your right. Head straight across to the opposite stile.

At this next stile head across the field towards the new houses, towards the stile in the left hand corner of the field. Cross over and continue along the bottom of the next field.

Shortly you reach another stile and gateway. Head right and cut diagonally left across the field to the far corner. At the next stile head along the right hand edge of the field. Shortly after the Golf Course comes into view watch out for a stile on your right.

5 Once on the Golf Course turn left along the hedgerow and then just past the second of two large oaks turn right across the fairway. On reaching the other side turn left keeping the hedge on your right.

At the end of the fairway, cross a stile and turn left through two small paddocks. On entering the third field turn right to a stile visible in the hedgerow. This leads into a lane which shortly emerges on the main road in the village. Turn left to return to the pub.

THE TITLEY LOOP

Distance: 3 miles (5 km)

Terrain: There is a continuous climb to Burnt House.

Access: Titley has a limited bus service from Kington. Car access by way of the B4355 between Kington and Presteigne.

Refreshment: The Stagg Inn, Titley.

Commencing at Titley Village Hall...

1 Starting from the Village Hall, turn left along the road and then at the T-Junction turn left again past the pub. Just past the Church turn left off the road joining the main spine of the Mortimer Trail.

According to folklore, water from the roadside well by the church was said to have medicinal properties. Unfortunately it is no longer regarded fit for consumption.

Continue up the headland of the next two fields. At the top of the second field the hedgerow swings around to the left. Follow this around and shortly there is a gap in the hedge on your right. Pass through this and cross another two fields heading towards the left hand corner of the second field. Turn left into the lane, and then immediately right past some farm buildings.

2 Continue on this track along the ridge, passing through two field gates and then just past an old stone barn turn left, keeping the hedgerow on your right. Follow this narrow wooded strip down until it again emerges into the field, this time keeping the hedgerow on your left. Where the remainder of the hedgerow turns sharp left, head diagonally right down to the bottom of the field. Pass through the gateway and head straight on to a stile in the hedgerow opposite. At the next stile the path continues more or less straight on to the gateway.

3 At this gate turn left towards the next gateway where the path joins a track which leads down to the road. Turn right at the road and follow this for about a quarter of a mile until you reach the village hall.

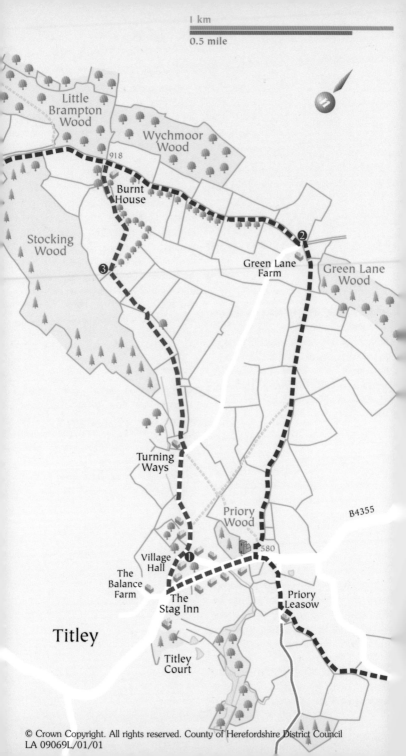

1 km

0.5 mile

Little
Brampton
Wood

Wychmoor
Wood

918

Burnt
House

Stocking
Wood

③

Green Lane
Farm

② Green Lane
Wood

Turning
Ways

Priory
Wood

B4355

580

Village
Hall

①

The
Balance
Farm

The
Stag Inn

Priory
Leasow

Titley

Titley
Court

WALKER'S SURVEY

We want to make sure that walking the Mortimer Trail is as safe and enjoyable as possible. Once you have walked as much of the walk as you intend, we would be very grateful if you could spare a few minutes to complete and return this reply paid card.

Please indicate how many people walked the trail with you.

☐ Walked as an individual

☐ Walked as a party.

Please enter size of party: ▢ Adults ▢ Children ▢ Dogs

☐ Were any members of the party mobility impaired?

If YES how did they cope with the route?

How many days have you spent walking the Mortimer Trail?

☐ Did you walk the Trail from end to end in one go?

If YES how many days did it take?

☐ Did you walk from Ludlow to Kington? ☐ Or Kington to Ludlow?

☐ Did you walk the Trail from end to end at different times?

If YES, how many days in total?

☐ Did you just walk selected sections?

If YES, approximately how many miles?

When did you walk the Mortimer Trail?

Approximately, how much in total did you/your party spend while walking the Mortimer Trail?

▢ Accommodation ▢ Refreshments ▢ Transport

How would you rate the overall experience offered by the Mortimer Trail?

☐ Very Good ☐ Good ☐ Fair ☐ Poor ☐ Very Poor

How did you learn about the Mortimer Trail?

What improvements would you like to see on the Mortimer Trail?

HEREFORDSHIRE
COUNCIL

Herefordshire Council
Parks & Countryside Service
FREEPOST SWC2983
PO BOX 41
LEOMINSTER
HR6 0ZZ